NOVEMBERLAND

ALSO BY GÜNTER GRASS

The Tin Drum

Cat and Mouse

Dog Years

The Plebeians Rehearse the Uprising

Four Plays

Speak Out!

Local Anaesthetic

Mac: A Play

From the Diary of a Snail

Inmarypraise

In the Egg and Other Poems

The Flounder

The Meeting at Telgte

Headbirths

Drawings and Words 1954–1977

On Writing and Politics 1967–1983

Etchings and Words 1972–1982

The Rat

Show Your Tongue

Two States—One Nation?

The Call of the Toad

GÜNTER GRASS

NOVEMBERLAND

Selected Poems 1956-1993

Translated from the German

by Michael Hamburger

A HELEN AND KURT WOLFF BOOK

A HARVEST ORIGINAL

HARCOURT BRACE & COMPANY

San Diego   New York   London

Library of Congress Cataloging-in-Publication Data
Grass, Günter, 1927-
Novemberland: selected poems, 1956-1993/Günter Grass;
translated by Michael Hamburger.—1st ed.
p.   cm.
"A Helen and Kurt Wolff book."
"A Harvest original."
ISBN 0-15-100177-4.—ISBN 0-15-600331-7 (pbk.)
1. Grass, Günter, 1927- —Translations into English.
I. Hamburger, Michael. II. Title.
PT2613.R338N6813   1996
831'.914—dc20   95-38418

Text set in Old Style 7
Designed by Lori J. McThomas
Printed in the United States of America
First edition
A B C D E

CONTENTS

Liebe Geprüft 1974

FROM *Der Butt 1977*

Miscellany

Novemberland 1993

FROM

Die Vorzüge der Windhühner

1956

POLNISCHE FAHNE

Viel Kirschen die aus diesem Blut
im Aufbegehren deutlich werden,
das Bett zum roten Inlett überreden.

Der erste Frost zählt Rüben, blinde Teiche,
Kartoffelfeuer überm Horizont,
auch Männer halb im Rauch verwickelt.

Die Tage schrumpfen, Äpfel auf dem Schrank,
die Freiheit fror, jetzt brennt sie in den Öfen,
kocht Kindern Brei und malt die Knöchel rot.

Im Schnee der Kopftücher beim Fest,
Pilsudskis Herz, des Pferdes fünfter Huf,
schlug an die Scheune, bis der Starost kam.

Die Fahne blutet musterlos,
so kam der Winter, wird der Schritt
hinter den Wölfen Warschau finden.

FLAG OF POLAND

Plenty of cherries that from this blood
in wishing's upsurge become clear,
persuade the bed to be an inlet, red.

First frost counts turnips, ponds gone blind,
potato fires above the horizon
and men half tangled in the smoke.

The days are shrinking, apples on the cupboard,
liberty froze, now it burns in the stoves,
cooks porridge for children and paints ankles red.

In the snow of headshawls at the fête
Pilsudski's heart, the fifth hoof of the horse,
knocked on the barn till the Starosty came.

The flag is bleeding patternless,
so winter came, the plodding steps
behind the wolves will find Warsaw.

LAMENTO BEI GLATTEIS

Sanna Sanna.
Meiner Puppe trocknes Innen,
meiner Sanna Sägespäne
hingestreut, weil draußen Glatteis,
Spiegel üben laut Natur.
Weil die Tanten, die nach Backobst,
auch Muskat, nach dem Kalender,
süß nach Futteralen riechen.
Weil die Tanten in den schwarzen,
lederweiten Blumentöpfen
welken und Gewicht verlieren.
Sanna Sanna, weil die Tanten
stürzen könnten, weil doch Glatteis,
könnten brechen überm Spiegel,
zweimal doppelt, Töpfe, Blumen.
Offen würden Futterale
und Kalender, kurz nach Lichtmeß,
der Vikar mit blauen Wangen
weihte Kerzen und den Schoß.

Späne nicht, so nehmt doch Asche.
Nur weil Tanten, meiner Sanna
ungekränktes, trocknes Innen
mit dem Schweiß der Spiegel nässen.
Sanna nein. Der Duft um Kerne
aufgetan, das Bittre deutlich,
so als wär der Kern die Summe
und Beweis, daß Obst schon Sünde.

LAMENT ON BLACK ICE

Sanna, Sanna.
My doll's dry inside,
my Sanna's sawdust
spilled, because black ice outside,
mirrors play at being nature.
Because the aunts who smell
of dried fruit, or musk,
of calendar, or sweetly
too of spectacle cases.
Because aunts in their all-black
leather-yawning flowerpots
wither and are losing weight.
Sanna, Sanna, because the aunts
could fall down, because black ice,
and above the mirror break,
twice over, doubly, pots and flowers.
Spectacle cases then would open
calendars too, just after Candlemas,
the vicar with his bluish cheeks
blessed the candles and their laps.

No, not sawdust. Please take ashes.
Only because aunts are moistening
my dear Sanna's unoffended,
dry inside with sweat of mirrors.
Sanna, no. The scent round pips
all opened up, the bitterness clear,
just as though the pip alone were
final proof that fruit are sin.

Aufgetan, nein Sanna schließe
dein Vertrauen, dein Geschlecht.
Gäb der Winter seine Nieren,
seine graue alte Milz
und sein Salz auf beide Wege.
Könnt dann Sanna, deine, Sanna,
hingestreute Puppenseele
Lerchen in Verwahrung geben.
Sanna Sanna.

Opened up, no, Sanna, close
both your trust now and your sex.
O, if winter gave its kidneys
and its gray and aged spleen,
and its salt on both our errands.
Then I could give Sanna, Sanna,
your own Sanna, scattered doll's soul
to the larks for safer keeping.
Sanna, Sanna.

PROPHETENKOST

Als Heuschrecken unsere Stadt besetzten,
keine Milch mehr ins Haus kam, die Zeitung erstickte,
öffnete man die Kerker, gab die Propheten frei.
Nun zogen sie durch die Straßen, 3800 Propheten.
Ungestraft durften sie reden, sich reichlich nähren
von jenem springenden, grauen Belag, den wir die Plage

nannten.
Wer hätte es anders erwartet.—

Bald kam uns wieder die Milch, die Zeitung atmete auf,
Propheten füllten die Kerker.

PROPHETS' FARE

When locusts occupied our city
no more milk reached our houses, the newspaper choked,
the prison cells were opened, the prophets set free.
Now they moved through the streets in procession, 3,800 prophets.
They could speak with impunity, and eat their fill
of that jumping, gray surface cover
that we called the plague.

Who would have expected any other outcome—

Soon the milk came back to us, the newspaper found its breath,
prophets filled the prison cells.

STREIT

Vier Vögel stritten.
Als kein Blatt mehr am Baum war,
kam Venus, verkleidet als Bleistift,
und hat den Herbst,
einen bald darauf fälligen Wechsel,
mit schöner Schrift unterschrieben.

QUARREL

Four birds quarreled.
When no leaf remained on the tree
Venus came, disguised as a pencil
and, in a beautiful script
signed autumn,
a conversion that soon would fall due.

BAUARBEITEN

Vor einer Woche kamen die Maurer
und brachten mit, was verlangt.
Sie haben ihn eingemauert,
den Hahn, den wir vermeiden wollten.—
Durch welchen Zufall kriecht dieser Ton?
Heute, noch immer erkalten die Suppen.
Fröstelnd stehen wir abseits und sehen den Hennen zu,
wenn sie den Mörtel vermindern.
Verlangen sie etwa nach Kalk?

CONSTRUCTION WORK

A week ago the bricklayers came
and brought with them what was required.
They have walled him in,
the rooster we wanted to avoid.
Through what accident does this sound creep?
Even today all our soups go cold.
Shivering we stand aside, watching the hens
as they diminish the mortar.
Could it be lime that they want?

V, DER VOGEL

V, der Vogel, ein Keil
dazwischengetrieben, als gelte es einen Himmel zu spalten,
als sei der Himmel Brennholz,
der Winter nahe, Brikett zu teuer,
ein Vogel eine geflügelte Axt.

V, der Vogel, ein Keil
den Urwald Blau Schlag auf Schlag abzubauen,
als kleine Stücke im Keller zu stapeln,
ein Vorrat Himmel, der lange reicht,
sich zählen läßt und nie mehr bewölkt.

V, der Vogel, ein Keil,
der hinterläßt einen Kahlschlag,
rodet auch und zwingt die Wurzel zum Zweifel.
Erst Feuer, der andere Vogel,
forstet hier auf, erklärt den Himmel zur Schonung.

V, der Vogel, ein Keil.
Und wenn der Keil nun den Rahmen verläßt?
Was eben noch Bild schien, gemäßigt, erlaubt im Format,
wuchert nun, eine Tapete,
im kleinen Ausschnitt verkäuflich.

V, der Vogel, ein Keil
läßt einen Apfel reißen, er offenbart ein Gehirn,
fügt dem Gebirge die Schlucht ein,
hat keine Scham und Vorbeisehn,
öffnet Verstecke im Fleisch.

V FOR VOLANT BIRD

V for volant bird, a wedge
driven between, as though to split a sky,
as though the sky were firewood,
winter were near, briquettes too expensive,
a bird were a winged axe.

V for volant bird, a wedge
to demolish the jungle azure blow by blow,
and stack in the cellar piecemeal,
a store of sky that will last a long time,
can be counted and never again be clouded.

V for volant bird, a wedge
that leaves a withering blow behind,
makes clearings too, and forces the root to doubt.
Only fire, the other bird,
will reforest here, declared the sky a protected area.

V for volant bird, a wedge.
And what if the wedge leaves the frame?
What only now seemed a picture, measured, its format permitted,
now grows rank, a wallpaper
on sale in small samples.

V for volant bird, a wedge
makes an apple split, it reveals a brain,
adds a ravine to the mountain range,
has no shame, or looking the other way,
opens up hideouts in flesh.

V, der Vogel, ein Keil
drängt sich dazwischen,
Teilhaben nennt er dieses,
wenn er auf heiser politischen Plätzen
dem Redner das Ende vom Satz trennt.

V, der Vogel, ein Keil,
kommt immer durch,
doppelt wählt ihn das W,
Winston hebt die zwei Finger
und jeder weiß, was er meint.

V for volant bird, a wedge
pushes in between,
calling that participation
when in hoarsely political places
it cuts off the end of the speaker's sentence.

V for volant bird, a wedge
always gets through,
the W will elect it twice over,
Winston raises his two fingers
and everyone knows what he means.

FROM

Gleisdreieck

1960

KINDERLIED

Wer lacht hier, hat gelacht?
Hier hat sich's ausgelacht.
Wer hier lacht, macht Verdacht,
daß er aus Gründen lacht.

Wer weint hier, hat geweint?
Hier wird nicht mehr geweint.
Wer hier weint, der auch meint,
daß er aus Gründen weint.

Wer spricht hier, spricht und schweigt?
Wer schweigt, wird angezeigt.
Wer hier spricht, hat verschwiegen,
wo seine Gründe liegen.

Wer spielt hier, spielt im Sand?
Wer spielt, muß an die Wand,
hat sich beim Spiel die Hand
gründlich verspielt, verbrannt.

Wer stirbt hier, ist gestorben?
Wer stirbt, ist abgeworben.
Wer hier stirbt, unverdorben
ist ohne Grund verstorben.

NURSERY RHYME

Who laughs here, who has laughed?
Here we have ceased to laugh.
To laugh here now is treason.
The laugher has a reason.

Who weeps here, who has wept?
Here weeping is inept.
To weep here now means too
a reason so to do.

Who speaks here or keeps mum?
Here we denounce the dumb.
To speak here is to hide
deep reasons kept inside.

Who plays here, in the sand?
Against the wall we stand
players whose games are banned.
They've lost, they've burned their hand.

Who dies here, dares to die?
"Defector!" here we cry.
To die here, without stain,
is to have died in vain.

DIE VOGELSCHEUCHEN

Ich weiß nicht, ob man Erde kaufen kann,
ob es genügt, wenn man vier Pfähle,
mit etwas Rost dazwischen und Gestrüpp,
im Sand verscharrt und Garten dazu sagt.

Ich weiß nicht, was die Stare denken.
Sie flattern manchmal auf, zerstäuben,
besprenkeln meinen Nachmittag,
tun so, als könnte man sie scheuchen,
als seien Vogelscheuchen Vogelscheuchen
und Luftgewehre hinter den Gardinen
und Katzen in der Bohnensaat.

Ich weiß nicht, was die alten Jacken
und Hosentaschen von uns wissen.
Ich weiß nicht, was in Hüten brütet,
welchen Gedanken was entschlüpft
und flügge wird und läßt sich nicht verscheuchen;
von Vogelscheuchen werden wir behütet.

Sind Vogelscheuchen Säugetiere?
Es sieht so aus, als ob sie sich vermehren,
indem sie nachts die Hüte tauschen:
schon stehn in meinem Garten drei,
verneigen sich und winken höflich
und drehen sich und zwinkern mit der Sonne
und reden, reden zum Salat.

THE SCARECROWS

I don't know whether earth can be bought,
whether it's enough to bury four posts,
with a little rust between them and some shrubs,
in the sand, and call the thing a garden.

I don't know what the starlings think.
Sometimes they flutter up, disperse,
sprinkle my afternoon,
pretend that one can scare them off,
as though scarecrows were scarecrows
and air guns behind the curtains
and cats in the beanrows.

I don't know what the old jackets
and those trouser pockets know about us.
I don't know what broods inside hats,
for what thoughts something is hatched,
and fledges and won't let itself be scared off;
by scarecrows in any case we are guarded.

Are scarecrows mammals?
It does look as though they multiplied
by swapping hats overnight:
already three of them stand in my garden,
bow, and politely wave to me
and turn about and wink at the sun
and talk, talk to the lettuces.

Ich weiß nicht, ob mein Gartenzaun
mich einsperren, mich aussperrn will.
Ich weiß nicht, was das Unkraut will,
weiß nicht, was jene Blattlaus will bedeuten,
weiß nicht, ob alte Jacken, alte Hosen,
wenn sie mit Löffeln in den Dosen
rostig und blechern windwärts läuten,
zur Vesper, ob zum Ave läuten,
zum Aufstand aller Vogelscheuchen läuten.

I don't know whether my garden fence
wants to shut me in or out.
I don't know what the weeds want,
don't know what that greenfly signifies,
don't know whether old jackets, old trousers
when with their spoons rusty and tinny
windward they ring, to vespers or ave they ring
or to the insurrection of every scarecrow.

ZAUBEREI MIT DEN BRÄUTEN CHRISTI

Aus himmlischen Töpfen

Wer hat dieses Spielchen ausgedacht?
Die Köche springen in den Hof,
erschrecken die Nonnen
oder auf Treppen fassen sie zu,
im Keller, im Speicher,
auf Gängen atemlos,
Hände behaart,
mit Löffeln schlagen sie
und rühren auf,
was gerade sich setzte,
und schöpfen ab, was ihm galt—
dem Bräutigam.

Theater

Köche, Nonnen und Vögel,
dann Wind aus der Kulisse,
und ganz am Anfang bricht ein Glas,
daß Scherben noch genug sind, wenn am Ende
die Nonnen flüchten—Kurs Südost.—
Auch Vögel kommen meistens in den Himmel,
weil sie den Köchen und dem Wind
an Federn überlegen sind.

MAGICAL EXERCISE WITH THE BRIDES OF CHRIST

Out of Celestial Pots

Who thought up this little game?
The chefs leap into the courtyard,
startle the nuns
or grab at them on the staircase,
in the cellar, in the attic,
in passages, breathless,
with hairy hands
with spoons they beat
and stir up
what was about to settle,
and skim off what concerned him—
the Bridegroom.

Theater

Chefs, nuns and birds,
then a wind from the wings
and right at the beginning a glass breaks
so that there are shards enough when at the end
the nuns take flight—their course southeasterly.
Birds too usually go to Heaven,
because in plumage they are superior
to chefs and the wind.

Vorsicht

Ergingen Nonnen sich am Strand
und hielten mit gewaschnen Händen
schwarz Regenschirme,
daß die Hitze
nicht Einfalt bräune.—
Kleine Füße traten Muscheln,
daß kein Ohr sei,
wenn Agneta, die Novize, sich verspräche,
was oft vorkommt.

Keine Taube

Es begegneten sich eine Möwe
und eine Nonne.
Und die Möwe
hackte der Nonne die Augen aus.
Die Nonne aber hob ihren Schleier,
lud wie Maria den Wind ein,
segelte blind und davon.—
Blieb der katholische Strand,
glaubte an blendende Segel,
Muschel rief Muschel ins Ohr:
Geliebte im Herrn und am Strand,
erschien ihr der heilige Geist
auch nicht in Gestalt einer Taube,
so schlug er doch weiß, daß ich glaube.

Caution

Nuns disported themselves on the beach
and in washed hands held
black umbrellas,
so that the heat
would not tan innocence.
Little feet trod on shells,
so that there would be no ear
when Agneta, the novice, stumbled over words
as she often does.

No Dove

A seagull and a nun
met.
And the seagull
hacked out the nun's eyes.
But the nun lifted her veil,
like Mary invited the wind,
blindly sailed up and away—
What remained was the Catholic beach,
it believed in dazzling sails,
seashell cried into seashell's ear:
Beloved in the Lord and on the beach,
if not in the guise of a dove
yet the Holy Spirit appeared to her,
and white those wings beat, so that I may believe.

Die Nonnen

Sie sind nur für den Wind gemacht.
Sie segeln immer, ohne auch zu loten.
Was ihnen himmlisch Bräutigam,
heißt andernorts Klabautermann.
Ich sah einst Nonnen,
eine ganze Flotte.
Sie wehten fort zum Horizont.
Ein schöner Tag, ein Segeltag,
tags drauf Trafalgar, die Armada sank.
Was wußte Nelson schon von Nonnen.

The Nuns

They are made for the wind.
They always sail, even without sounding the depth.
What to them is the Celestial Bridegroom
elsewhere is known as the Ship's Hobgoblin.
I once saw nuns,
a whole fleet of them.
They wafted off to the horizon.
A fine day, a day for sailing,
the day after, Trafalgar, the Armada sank.
What, after all, did Nelson know about nuns.

RACINE LÄSST SEIN WAPPEN ÄNDERN

Ein heraldischer Schwan
und eine heraldische Ratte
bilden—oben der Schwan,
darunter die Ratte—
das Wappen des Herrn Racine.

Oft sinnt Racine
über dem Wappen und lächelt,
als wüßte er Antwort,
wenn Freunde nach seinem Schwan fragen,
aber die Ratte meinen.

Es steht Racine
einem Teich daneben
und ist auf Verse aus,
die er kühl und gemessen
mittels Mondlicht und Wasserspiegel verfertigen kann.

Schwäne schlafen
dort wo es seicht ist,
und Racine begreift jenen Teil seines Wappens,
welcher weiß ist
und der Schönheit als Kopfkissen dient.

Es schläft aber die Ratte nicht,
ist eine Wasserratte
und nagt, wie Wasserratten es tun,
von unten mit Zähnen
den schlafenden Schwan an.

RACINE HAS HIS COAT OF ARMS ALTERED

A heraldic swan
and a heraldic rat
form—the swan above,
the rat below—
M. Racine's coat of arms.

Often Racine ponders
his coat of arms and smiles,
as though he knew the answer
when friends ask about the swan
but mean the rat.

Racine is standing
next to a pond,
out for verses
which he can produce
cool and measured, by means of moonlight and reflecting surface.

Swans are asleep
where it's shallow,
and Racine understands that part of his coat of arms
which is white
and serves beauty as a pillow.

But the rat is not asleep,
it's a water rat
and it gnaws, as water rats will,
from down below with teeth
at the sleeping swan.

Auf schreit der Schwan,
das Wasser reißt,
Mondlicht verarmt und Racine beschließt,
nach Hause zu gehen,
sein Wappen zu ändern.

Fort streicht er die heraldische Ratte.
Die aber hört nicht auf, seinem Wappen zu fehlen.
Weiß stumm und rattenlos
wird der Schwan seinen Einsatz verschlafen—
Racine entsagt dem Theater.

The swan cries out,
the water rips,
moonlight grows poor and Racine decides
to go home
and alter his coat of arms.

He deletes the heraldic rat
but it never ceases to be missed from his coat of arms.
White mute and ratless
the swan will oversleep its entrance—
Racine gives up the theater.

GEFLÜGEL AUF DEM ZENTRALFRIEDHOF

Meine Hühner lachen nicht.
Kaum unterscheidet sich ihr Gerüst
vom Efeu und anderen Kletterpflanzen,
dazwischen ein Grabstein
immer denselben Namen
Silbe um Silbe flüstert,
wie Kinder ein schweres Gedicht . . .

Meine Hühner lachen nicht,
messen die Vierecke aus,
ordnen verflossene Schleifen,
stehen, Portale zwischen den Gräbern,
der Kundschaft entgegen,
der schwarzen, sich räuspernden Raupe,
die zögernd, den Hut in der Hand,
das Kästchen bringt voller kaltem
witzlosem Fleisch für die Hühner.

Seht Ihr den Hahn
auf dem Spaten in lockerer Erde?
Manchmal singt er und hackt
bronzene Späne vom Glöckchen.
Draußen hinter den Ulmen,
im Gasthaus zu Pietät,
taucht der Humor seinen Finger
in ein Glas Bier und rührt und rührt . . .

Meine Hühner lachen nicht.

POULTRY IN THE CENTRAL CEMETERY

My hens do not cackle.
Their scaffolding hardly differs
from ivy and other climbing plants,
in between, a gravestone
syllable by syllable whispers
always the same name,
as children will a difficult poem . . .

My hens do not cackle,
they survey the rectangles,
tidy bows that have slipped,
as portals between the graves
they stand, facing the client,
the black caterpillar clearing its throat
who hesitant, hat in hand,
brings the small box full of cold
witless meat for the hens.

Do you see the rooster
on that spade in loosened soil?
Sometimes he sings and hacks
bronze chips from the little bell.
Outside, behind the elms
in the Piety Inn,
Humor dips his finger
in a glass of beer and stirs and stirs . . .

My hens do not cackle.

DIE GARDINENPREDIGT

Die aus den Beichtstühlen klettern:
halbverbrauchte Athleten,
draußen vor dem Portal
schnappen sie wieder nach Luft,
wollen
—als wäre das üblich—
mit einer Sonne boxen
oder den Regen verbiegen.

Doch süßer als Bier,
teurer als kleine gefüllte Frauen,
sterblicher noch als Tabak
ist es, den Urlaub,
die wenigen gottlosen Tage
bei den Gardinen,
im Garten Tüll
zu verbringen.

Langstreckenläufer
ruhen hier aus,
finden in jeder mystischen Masche
Trost und Verzeihen;
so jene Fliege von gestern,
trocken, ohne Begehren,
hält nur noch still:
ein neuer Anteil Gardine.

Dann und wann Mücken,
nahe Verwandte der Engel,

THE CURTAIN SERMON

Those who climb out of the confessionals:
half-used-up athletes,
outside, in front of the portal
they gasp for air again,
want—
as though that were usual—
to box with a sun
or bend the rain.

But sweeter than beer,
dearer than small stuffed women,
more mortal still than tobacco
it is to spend
one's vacation,
these few godless days
with the curtains
in the garden of tulle.

Long-distance runners
rest here,
find in every mystical mesh
comfort and forgiveness;
like yesterday's fly,
dried-out, without desire,
that only keeps still:
a new share of the curtain.

From time to time midges,
close relatives of angels,

ein Wort,
das dem Radio entrinnt,
vom Wasserstand spricht und vom Wetter,
vom nahen Hurrikan ROSA,
der sich uns nähert und nähert,
doch immer noch weit ist, weit weg.

Sagt nicht: Oh Gott
—das gilt hier nicht—sagt:
Heiliger billiger Vorhang,
süße welke Gardine,
du hast den Honig erfunden,
die gaumenlos Freude der Irren,
die frühen Laute Perlmutter—
nimm mich nun auf.

Wer wollte Erlösung,
rief nach dem Arzt oder nach Milch?
Nun kommen sie: Priester und Ambulanzen,
Krankenschwestern und Nonnen.
Mit Sprüchen und Karbol,
mit Orgel und Äther,
mit Brillen und Latein vermessen sie mein Jenseits,
verbrennen sie meine Gardinen.

a word
that escapes the radio
speaks of water levels and weather,
of the approaching hurricane Rosa,
that gets closer and closer to us,
yet is still far away, far away.

Do not say: O God
—that's not valid here—say:
Holy cheap curtain,
sweet withered curtain,
thou hast invented honey,
the palateless pleasure of madmen,
the early sounds mother-of-pearl—
receive me now.

Who wanted redemption,
called for the doctor or milk?
Now they come: priests and ambulances,
nurses and nuns.
With spiritual texts and carbolic,
with organ and ether,
with spectacles and with Latin they survey my afterlife,
and burn my curtains.

ZWISCHEN MARATHON UND ATHEN

Die Henne wohnt auf leisen Eiern
und brütet über Start und Ziel.
Die Sonne läuft, besetzt ist die Tribüne
im Schatten, doch die Sonne läuft.

Von Rot verfolgt, um Mittag ohne Schuhe,
durch ein Spalier Konservendosen,
aus denen Löffel Beifall kratzen—
den ersten Rost und letztes Fett.

Vorbei an einem Bündel Präsidenten
mit Gattinnen in Pergament,
drauf Glückwünsche, zart steil geschrieben:
Wir freuen uns—Wir freuen uns . . .

Worauf denn? Glaubt wer noch an Siege?
An einen Boten, der auf halbgeschmolznen Beinen
ans Ziel kommt, seinem Kanzler stottert:
Sieg, Bonn war eine Messe wert!

Die Strecke stottert Fahnenmaste,
die Fahnen stottern und der Wind;
nur eine Schnecke spricht normal
und überrundet Zatopek.

BETWEEN MARATHON AND ATHENS

The hen resides upon her quiet eggs
and broods upon the start and goal.
The sun runs on, the grandstand's occupied
in shadow, but the sun runs on.

Pursued by red, at noon without its shoes,
a gauntlet of preserving cans
from which applause is scratched by spoons—
initial rust and final grease.

Past a conglomerate of presidents
with lady wives in parchment wraps,
on then, congratulations, steeply, finely penned:
We so look forward— So look forward . . .

To what, then? Who believes in victories now?
Or in a herald who on legs half melted
reaches his destination, gasps to his chancellor:
Victory, sir! Bonn was worth a Mass!

The track is stuttering flagpoles now,
the flags are stuttering, and the wind;
only a snail talks normally
and laps the runner Zatopek.

AUF WEISSEM PAPIER

Möbel in einen entleerten
heisergebrüllten Raum schieben
und nicht mehr ein Stühlchen verrücken.
Hühner an einem windigen Dreieck
anbinden und Futter streuen:
Dieses Körnchen Geometrie,
daran die Eier gesunden.

Auf weißem hellwachem Papier
in die Irre gehen
oder das Plätzchen finden,
da sonntags der Angler sitzt
mit dem unvermeidlichen Köder:
Anmut, Geld, Glück bei den Frauen,
eine Verabredung pünktlich
auf weißem Papier.

ON WHITE PAPER

To push furniture into
a vacated room, yelled hoarse,
and not shift another small chair.
Tie hens to a windy triangle
and scatter feed for them:
This little grain of geometry
that restores eggs to health.

On white wide-awake paper
to go astray
or find the little spot
where the angler sits on a Sunday
with his inevitable bait:
grace, money, luck with women,
an appointment punctual
on white paper.

DIE GROSSE TRÜMMERFRAU SPRICHT

Gnade Gnade.
Die große Trümmerfrau
hat einen Plan entworfen,
dem jeder Stein unterliegen wird.
Der große Ziegelbrenner will mitmachen.

Die Stadt die Stadt.
Hingestreut liegt Berlin,
lehnt sich mit Brandmauern gegen Winde,
die aus Ost Süd West, aus dem Norden kommen
und die Stadt befreien wollen.

Hier drüben hier
und drüben hängen die Herzen
an einem einzigen Bindfaden,
hüpfen und werden gehüpft, wenn Trümmerfrau
und Ziegelbrenner ihre Liebe zu Faden schlagen.

Liebe Liebe
spielten einst Trümmerfrauen,
rieben mit Schenkeln
Klinker und Ziegel
zu Splitt Mehl Staub Liebe.

Wo wo wo wo
sind die alten Galane geblieben,
wo wilhelminischer Mörtel?
Jahrgänge Jahrgänge—
doch Trümmerfrauen sind keine Weinkenner.

THE GREAT RUBBLEWOMAN SPEAKS:

Mercy mercy.
The great rubblewoman
has conceived a plan
to which every stone will have to submit
The great brickburner wants to join in.

Our city our city.
All scattered lies Berlin,
leans with its fire walls against winds
that come from east south west, and from the north,
wishing to liberate the city.

Here over there here
and over there hearts hang
by a single length of string,
hop and are hopped, when rubblewoman
and brickburner beat their love into threads.

Love love
at one time rubblewomen played at,
with their thighs rubbed
clinker and brick
into chippings flour dust love.

Where where where where
have the old gallants gone,
where Kaiser Wilhelm's mortar?
Vintage years vintage years—
but rubblewomen are no connoisseurs of wine.

Flaute Flaute
schreien die Trümmerfrauen
und lassen den letzten
wundertätigen Ziegelstein
zwischen den Zähnen knirschen.

Splitt Splitt Splitt Splitt.
Nur noch wenn Zwiebeln
oder ein kleineres Leid
uns mit Tränen versorgen,
tritt Ziegelsplitt aufs Augenlid.

Sonderbar sonderbar
sehen dann Neubauten aus,
zittern ein wenig, erwarten
den klassisch zu nennenden Schlag
mit der Handkante in die Kniekehle.

Sie sie sie sie
gräbt den Sand unterm Pfeiler weg.
Sie sag ich sie
spuckt in die trächtigen
Betonmischmaschinen.

Sie sie sie sie
hat das große Gelächter erfunden.
Wenn immer die große Trümmerfrau lacht,
klemmen Fahrstühle, springen Heizkörper,
weinen die kleinen verwöhnten Baumeister.

Stagnation stagnation
shriek the rubblewomen
and make the last
miraculous brick
grate between their teeth.

Chippings chippings chippings chippings
Only now when onions
or a smaller sorrow
supply us with tears
do fresh chippings touch our eyelids.

Strange strange
then the new buildings look,
tremble a little, await
the blow you'd call classical
with the side of the hand into the knee's hollow.

She she she she
digs away the sand under the pillar.
She I say she
spits into the pregnant
concrete mixers.

She she she she
has invented the great laughter.
Whenever the great rubblewoman laughs
elevators jam, radiators burst,
the small pampered architects weep.

Mir gab sie mir,
ihrem ängstlich beflissenen Ziegelersatz,
gab sie den Auftrag,
Wind zu machen, Staub zu machen
und ernsthaft für ihr Gelächter zu werben.

Ich ich ich ich
stand abseits,
hatte die Brandmauer im Auge,
und die Brandmauer
hatte mich im Auge.

Ging ging ging ging
von weit her
auf die Brandmauer los,
als wollte ich
die Brandmauer durchschreiten.

Nahm nahm nahm nahm
einen Anlauf,
der viel versprach;
jene Brandmauer aber war neunzehn Meter breit
und zweiundzwanzig Meter hoch.

Schlug schlug schlug schlug
an der Mauer
mein Wasser ab,
daß es rauschte
und hörte dem zu.

To me, to me she gave,
her timidly hardworking brick substitute,
she gave the commission
to make wind, to make dust
and seriously promote her laughter.

I I I I
stood aside,
kept my eye on the fire wall,
and the fire wall
kept its eye on me.

Went went went went
from far off
went for the fire wall,
as though I wanted
to walk through the fire wall.

Took took took took
a long run
that was most promising,
but that fire wall was nineteen meters wide
and twenty-two meters high.

Made made made made
water against
that wall,
so that it roared,
and listened to that.

Werbung Werbung
rauschte die Brandmauer.
Niemand will mich als Werbefläche
mieten, haushoch beschriften
und werben lassen.

Ich ich ich ich
will allen Brandmauern,
die nordwärts schauen,
riesengroß Trümmerfrauen
malen oder auch einbrennen.

Trümmerfrau Trümmerfrau
—sollen die Kinder singen—
hat mit dem Ziegelbrenner Ziegelbrenner
einen ganz neuen Plan gemacht.
Alle Steine wissen Bescheid.

Ziegelbrenner Ziegelbrenner
—sollen die Kinder singen—
geht nachts mit der Trümmerfrau Trümmerfrau
durch die Stadt
und schätzt die Stadt ab.

Trümmerfrau Trümmerfrau
—singen die Kinder—
will mit dem Ziegelbrenner Ziegelbrenner
heut eine Wette machen Wette machen—
es geht um viel Schutt.

Sales promotion sales promotion
the fire wall roared,
no one wants to hire me as
a billboard, letter me house-high
and let me promote sales.

I I I I
want to paint onto or burn
into all fire walls that face north
gigantic
rubblewomen.

Rubblewoman rubblewoman
—the children are to sing—
together with the brickburner brickburner
has hatched a wholly new plan
All the stones know all about it.

Brickburner brickburner
—the children are to sing—
at night walks with the rubblewoman rubblewoman
through the city
and assesses its value.

Rubblewoman rubblewoman
—the children sing—
with the brickburner brickburner
wants to lay a bet lay a bet today—
much rubble is at stake.

Lamento Lamento—
die große Trümmerfrau singt ihr Lamento.
Doch alle Sender, drüben und hier,
-senden von früh bis spät nur jenen alten
beschissenen Walzerkönig.

Tot sie ist tot
sagen die Baumeister,
verschweigen aber, daß eine unabwendbare Hand
Mittag für Mittag löffelweis toten Mörtel
in ihre Suppen mengt.

Amen Amen.
Hingestreut liegt Berlin.
Staub fliegt auf,
dann wieder Flaute.
Die große Trümmerfrau wird heiliggesprochen.

Lamentation lamentation—
the great rubblewoman sings her lamentation.
But all the radio stations, over there and here,
from morning to night only transmit
that shitty old king of waltzes.

Dead she is dead
the architects say,
but do not say that an ineluctable hand
noon after noon mixes by spoonfuls
dead mortar into their soups.

Amen Amen.
All scattered lies Berlin.
Dust flies up,
then stagnation again.
The great rubblewoman is canonized.

FROM

Ausgefragt

1967

JA

Neue Standpunkte fassen Beschlüsse
und bestehen auf Vorfahrt.
Regelwidrig geparkt, winzig,
vom Frost übersprungen,
nistet die Anmut.
Ihr ist es Mühsal, Beruf,
die Symmetrie zu zerlächeln:
Alles Schöne ist schief.
  Uns verbinden, tröste Dich,
  ansteckende Krankheiten.
  Ruhig atmen—so—
  und die Flucht einschläfern.
  Jeder Colt sagt entwederoder . . .
  Zwischen Anna und Anna
  entscheide ich mich für Anna.
Übermorgen ist schon gewesen.
Heute war wedernoch.
Was auf mich zukommt,
eingleisig,
liegt weiter zurück als Austerlitz.
Zu spät. Ich vergesse Zahlen,
bevor sie strammstehen.
  Grau ist die Messe.
  Denn zwischen Schwarz und Weiß,
  immer verängstigt,
  grämen sich Zwischentöne.
  Mein großes Ja
  bildet Sätze mit kleinem nein:

YES

New standpoints arrive at resolutions
and insist on right-of-way.
Parked against the rules, tiny,
leapfrogged by frost,
grace nests.
To her it's a burden, a calling,
to break symmetry with her smiles:
all beautiful things are awry.
    Take comfort, infectious diseases
    are a bond between us.
    Breathe quietly—so—
    and put flight to sleep.
    Every colt says eitheror . . .
    Between Anna and Anna
    it is Anna I choose.
The day after tomorrow is already over.
Today was neithernor.
What's coming toward me
on a single rail
lies farther behind me than Austerlitz.
Too late. I forget numbers
before they stand at attention.
    Gray the Mass is.
    For between black and white,
    always intimidated
    the quarter tones grieve.
    My great yes
    forms sentences with a small no:

Dieses Haus hat zwei Ausgänge;
ich benutze den dritten.
Im Negativ einer Witwe,
in meinem Ja liegt mein nein begraben.

This house has two exits;
I use the third.
In the negative of a widow,
in my yes my no lies buried.

SCHREIBEN

In Wirklichkeit
  war das Glas nur hüfthoch gefüllt.
    Vollschlank geneigt. Im Bodensatz liegt.
Silben stechen.
Neben dem Müllschlucker wohnen
und zwischen Gestank und Geruch ermitteln.
Dem Kuchen die Springform nehmen.
Bücher,
  in ihren Gestellen,
    können nicht umfallen.
Das, oft unterbrochen, sind meine Gedanken.
Wann wird die Milch komisch?
Im Krebsgang den Fortschritt messen.
Abwarten, bis das Metall ermüdet.
Die Brücke langsam.
  zum Mitschreiben,
    einstürzen lassen.
Vorher den Schrottwert errechnen.
Sätze verabschieden Sätze.
Wenn Politik
  dem Wetter
    zur Aussage wird:
Ein Hoch über Rußland.
Zuhause
  verreist sein; auf Reisen
  zuhause bleiben.
Wir wechseln das Klima nicht.
Nur Einfalt
  will etwas beleben,

WRITING

In reality
   the glass was filled only hip high.
      Plump, well-rounded. Lies in the dregs.
Engrave syllables.
Live next to the garbage disposal unit
and distinguish between a stench and a smell.
Deprive the cake of its springform.
Books
  in their cases
    can't fall over.
That, often interrupted, is how my thoughts went.
When does the milk grow funny?
Measure progress in crayfish gait.
Wait patiently until metal tires.
Let the bridge slowly,
  so that the writing keeps pace,
    collapse.
Before that, calculate its value as scrap.
Sentences bid farewell to sentences.
When politics
  become
    the weather's way of speaking:
A high-pressure belt over Russia.
At home
  to have gone abroad; on travels
  to remain at home.
We will not change the climate.
Only naïveté
  wants to make something live,

für tot erklären.

Dumm sein, immer neu anfangen wollen.

Erinnere mich bitte, sobald ich Heuschnupfen

oder der Blumenkorso in Zoppot sage.

Rückblickend aus dem Fenster schauen.

Reime auf Schnepfendreck.

Jeden Unsinn laut mitsprechen.

Urbin, ich hab's!—Urbin, ich hab's!

Das Ungenaue genau treffen.

Die Taschen

   sind voller alter Eintrittskarten.

      Wo ist der Zündschlüssel?

Den Zündschlüssel streichen.

Mitleid mit Verben.

An den Radiergummi glauben.

Im Fundbüro einen Schirm beschwören.

Mit der Teigrolle den Augenblick walzen.

Und die Zusammenhänge wieder auftrennen.

    Weil . . . wegen . . . als . . . damit . . . um . . .

      Vergleiche und ähnliche Alleskleber.

Diese Geschichte muß aufhören.

Mit einem Doppelpunkt schließen:

Ich komme wieder. Ich komme wieder.

Im Vakuum heiter bleiben.

Nur Eigenes stehlen.

Das Chaos

   in verbesserter Ausführung.

     Nicht schmücken—schreiben:

declare it dead.
Be stupid, always want to begin from scratch.
Please remind me as soon as I say
hay fever or the Corso of Flowers in Zoppot.
Retrospectively look out of the window.
Rhymes for snipes' droppings.
Loudly join in when anyone's talking nonsense.
Urbin, that's it!—Urbin, that's it!
Hit on the imprecise thing precisely.
Pockets
   are full of old admission tickets.
     Where is the car key?
Delete the car key.
Compassion with verbs.
Believe in the eraser.
Conjure an umbrella in the Lost and Found.
Bulldoze the moment with the rolling pin.
And take the connections apart again.
     Because . . . due to . . . when . . . so that . . . to . . .
     comparisons and similar adhesive aids.
This story must come to an end.
Conclude with a colon:
I'm coming back. I'm coming back.
Remain cheerful in a vacuum.
Steal only things of one's own.
Chaos
   more skillfully executed.
     Not adorn—write:

EFEU—DIE ZUWACHSRATE UNSTERBLICHKEIT

Ach. Einarmig früh schon
beschämte der Geiger
den doppelpfotigen Beifall.

Als er vor Jahresfrist plötzlich verstarb,
wurde uns seine Verbeugung,
dieser Winkel, die Fallsucht zu messen,
zum steingehauenen Maß.

Das nämlich,
wachsende Zuneigung,
hatte er uns voraus.
Nicht nur als Denkmal, zu Lebzeiten schon,
wie diesem Marmor heute,
hinkte auch ihm
fatal die bedeutende Schulter.

Doch was sich neigt, muß nicht stürzen.
Nie wird sein Name platt aufs Gesicht.
Ihm wächst die Ranke:

hilfreich kletternde Pflanze,
die seinen Überhang lindert,
bis sich das Lotrechte
schiefgelacht hat.

Das nämlich, Efeu,
die Zuwachsrate Unsterblichkeit,
hatte er uns voraus.

IVY—THE GROWTH RATE OF IMMORTALITY

Ah. One-armed quite early on
the violinist put to shame
the two-pawed applause.

When he suddenly died before the year was out,
his bow, that angle gauge
for the falling sickness, became for us
a measure hewn in stone.

For it was in this,
a growing inclination,
that he surpassed us.
Not as a monument only, but in his lifetime
as this marble does now,
his distinguished shoulder too
fatally limped.

But things that incline need not collapse.
Never will his name be flat on his face.
The creeper grows for him:

helpfully climbing plant
that allays his drapery
until the vertical
has laughed itself crooked.

For it was in this, ivy,
the growth rate of immortality,
that he surpassed us.

DOPPELPORTRAIT

der Fotografin Renate Höllerer gewidmet

Alle Köpfe im Ausschnitt gewinnen.
Wenn ein Hai im Profil durch das Bild schwimmt.
Oder auch Haare extra bei Gegenwind.
Nimm dich zusammen: Postkartengröße.

In meinem Motivsucher stellte sich ein:
ich, die linke gefällige Seite
ausgeleuchtet nach der Rasur
und straff, weil geohrfeigt.

Wenn immer mein Hündchen bellt,
mache ich knips und belichte:
Dich und den Hintergrund.
Meine Geliebte ertrinkt im Entwickler.

Schwarz. Das sind wir auf zwei Stühlen,
wenn wir schweigen, dem Auslöser lauschen:
breit im Format, bei angehaltenem Atem
und verdeckter Blende.

DOUBLE PORTRAIT
dedicated to the photographer Renate Höllerer

Every head gains by being cut out.
If a shark in profile swims through the picture.
Or hair, too, as an extra, against the wind.
Pull yourself together: postcard size.

In my motive finder there appeared:
myself, the left, affable side
photo-flooded after shaving
and taut, because it had been slapped.

Whenever my little dog barks
I go click and use the flash:
on you and the background.
In the developer my loved one drowns.

Black. That's us on our two chairs,
when we're silent, listening to the release:
wide in format, with our breath held
and the diaphragm covered.

DIE ERSTGEBURT

Dann werde ich meinen Söhnen Linsen kochen.
Der Vater, der kann das.
Dann werden sie handeln;
und jener wird Esau sein,
der seinen Vater liebt und seines Vaters Küche.

THE FIRSTBORN

Then I shall cook lentil soup for my sons.
Our dad, he's good at that.
Then they will do business;
and that one will be Esau
who loves his father and his father's cooking.

TOUR DE FRANCE

Als die Spitzengruppe
von einem Zitronenfalter
überholt wurde,
gaben viele Radfahrer das Rennen auf.

TOUR DE FRANCE

When the leading bunch
were overtaken
by a brimstone butterfly
many cyclists gave up the race.

SONNTAGMORGEN

Wie sie zärtlich in sich gekehrt,
ernst besorgt um den fingerlang Kratzer,
ihren Wagen
und seine Stoßstange waschen.

SUNDAY MORNING

How lovingly turned in on themselves,
gravely concerned about the finger-long scratch,
they wash
their car and its bumper.

DEKADENZ

Obgleich frische Eier Aspirin enthalten,
haben die Hähne Kopfschmerzen,
treten aber trotzdem;
wie nervös die Küken im Frühjahr ausschlüpfen.

DECADENCE

Although new-laid eggs contain aspirin,
the cocks have a headache,
but tread the hens all the same;
how nervously the chicks hatch in the spring.

DIE PEITSCHE

Weil jeder Leiche etwas entsprießt,
weil keine Haut dicht
und kein Geheimnis niet- oder nagelfest ist,
fängt langsam an wie das Gold
der Frühling unter dem Schnee.

Noch schläft die Peitsche und in der Peitsche
aufgerollt der April.
Noch sägt jemand Holz, denkt dabei an den Winter;
und eine Frau geht vorbei,
doch er dreht sich nicht um.

Ein Junge steht auf dem Hof,
schielt und hält eine Peitsche.
Dann dreht er sich langsam, dreht
und schielt nicht mehr, nein er dreht
und knallt haushock mit der Peitsche.

THE WHIP

Because something sprouts from every corpse,
because no skin is airtight
and no secret is burglarproof,
slow as gold
spring begins under the snow.

Still the whip sleeps and in the whip
April, rolled up.
Still someone saws logs, thinking of winter,
and a woman passes,
but he doesn't turn his head.

A boy stands in the yard,
squints and holds a whip.
Then he slowly turns, turns around
and no longer squints, no, he turns
and house-high cracks his whip.

GESAMTDEUTSCHER MÄRZ

Gustav Steffen zum Andenken

Die Krisen sprießen, Knospen knallen,
in Passau will ein Biedermann
den Föhn verhaften, Strauß beteuert,
daß er nicht schuld sei, wenn es taut;
in Bayern wird viel Bier gebraut.

Der Schnee verzehrt sich, Ulbricht dauert.
Gesamtdeutsch blüht der Stacheldraht.
Hier oder drüben, liquidieren
wird man den Winter laut Beschluß:
die Gärtner stehn Gewehr bei Fuß.

In Schilda wird ein Hochhaus, fensterlos,
das Licht verhüten; milde Lüfte
sind nicht gefragt, der alte Mief
soll konservieren Würdenträger
und Prinz Eugen, den Großwildjäger.

Im Friedenslager feiert Preußen
das Osterfest, denn auferstanden
sind Stechschritt und Parademarsch;
die Tage der Kommune sind vorbei,
und Marx verging im Leipz'ger Allerlei.

Bald wärmt die Sonne und der greise,
schon legendäre Fuchs verläßt
zum Kirchgang-Wahlkampf seinen Bau;

UNITED GERMANY FESTIVAL, MARCH
in memory of Gustav Steffen

Crises are sprouting, buds exploding,
an upright Passau citizen wants
the *föhn* arrested, Strauss insists
it's not his fault if there's a thaw;
Bavarian brewery profits soar.

Snow's losing heart, but Ulbricht holding.
Barbed wire, United-German, blooms.
The winter will be liquidated
by resolutions here and there:
gardeners await the order: fire!

A windowless high-rise block at Schilda
will keep out light; the milder breezes
are not in demand. The old, stale air
will do for dignitaries, and sustain
the big-game hunter, Prince Eugene.

A peace camp Prussia is celebrating
Easter, that is, the resurrection
of goose step, ceremonial march;
days of the Commune are old hat,
and Marx got lost in Leipzig's this-and-that.

Soon sunshine will be warming and the old
already-legendary fox will leave
his earth for campaigning and churchgoing;

der Rhein riecht fromm nach Abendland,
und Globke lächelt aus dem Zeugenstand.

Heut gab es an der Grenze keinen Toten.
Nun langweilt sich das Bild-Archiv.
Seht die Idylle: Vogelscheuchen
sind beiderseits der Elbe aufmarschiert;
jetzt werden Spatzen ideologisiert.

O, Deutschland, Hamlet kehrte heim:
»Er ist zu fett und kurz von Atem . . .«
und will, will nicht, auf kleiner Flamme
verkocht sein Image: Pichelsteiner Topf;
die Bundesliga spielt um Yoricks Kopf.

Bald wird das Frühjahr, dann der Sommer
mit all den Krisen pleite sein,—
glaubt dem Kalender, im September
beginnt der Herbst, das Stimmenzählen;
ich rat Euch, Es-Pe-De zu wählen.

the Rhine smells piously of Western land
and Globke smiles from the witness stand.

Today there were no corpses at the border.
The picture archive now feels bored.
Look at the idyll: on both sides of the Elbe
scarecrows are marching, all differently disguised;
the sparrows, too, are ideologized.

O, Germany, it's Hamlet who's come home:
"He's fat, and scant of breath . . ."
and wants and does not want, on a low flame
his image stews and will evaporate.
The German team competes for Yorick's pate.

Soon will the spring and then the summer
with all these crises come to bankruptcy—
believe the calendar, for in September
autumn begins, vote-counts for you and me;
take my advice, elect the S.P.D.

Liebe Geprüft

1974

LIEBE GEPRÜFT

Dein Apfel—mein Apfel.
Jetzt beißen wir gleichzeitig zu:
schau, wie auf ewig verschieden.
Jetzt legen wir Apfel und Apfel
Biß gegen Biß.

LOVE TESTED

Your apple—my apple.
Now we bite at the same time:
look, how forever differently.
Now we lay apple to apple
bite beside bite.

DOCH ABER

Mit Brille neuerdings
mehr Pickel freundlicher sehen.

Im Ausschnitt befangen,
fältchengetreu (begabter für Liebe)
doch ohne Einsicht in jenen Zusammenhang,
den das Gebirge als Horizont diktiert.

Aber die eigenen brüchigen Nähte
sind mir jetzt näher.
Neu und entsetzt
sehe ich meinen Abfall
und wie die Linien wackeln.

BUT STILL

With spectacles lately
see more pimples more kindly.

Caught in the neckline
faithful to little wrinkles (more gifted for love)
but with no insight into that connection
which the mountain range dictates as horizon.

But my own brittle seams
are closer to me now.
Newly and horrified
I see my decline
and how the lines wobble.

DEIN OHR

Gutzureden wahrsagen.
Wollte mich ausgesprochen versenken.
Wollte verstanden sein dumm.
Nur zwischen Gänsefüßchen oder gedruckt
bleigefaßt lügen.

Was keinen Grund findet aber Antwort bekommt:
logische Ketten,
geständiges Flüstern,
die Pause ausgespart,
Sprachschotter Lautgeröll.

In den Wind gehißt,
flattert dein Ohr,
hört sich flattern.

Beim Fädeln spleißen die Wörter danebengesagt.

YOUR EAR

Soothingly reassure. Blandly tell fortune.
Wished to communicate deeply.
For my stupidity wanted your understanding.
Between quotation marks only or printed,
set in lead, to lie.

What finds no reason but receives an answer:
logical chains,
confessional whispering,
the interval kept in reserve,
speech-rubble sound-scree.

Hoisted into the wind
Your ear flutters,
hears itself flutter.

As I thread words they split, spoken off-target.

WIE OHNE VERNUNFT

Mein Zufall wirft:
Krabben und Kippen.
Auszählen jetzt,
den Wurf lesen
und deine und meine Hölzchen,
(die abgebrannten)
hier und dort
krisengerecht überkreuz legen.

AS THOUGH WITHOUT REASON

My chance throws down
shrimps, cigarette butts.
Now deal them counted,
interpret the throw,
lay your matchsticks and mine
(those burnt out),
here and there
crosswise to meet the crisis.

SCENISCHES MADRIGAL

Das trennt.
So nah wir liegen,
schwimmen doch Fische von anderen Küsten
dort, wo wir meinten,
uns trockengelegt zu haben.

Ähnlich getäuscht verläuft sich draußen,
was wir (noch immer) Gesellschaft nennen:
Frauen, die ihren Mann stehen,
verheulte Männer,
Tiere ohne Duftmarken und Adresse.

Auf unserer Langspielplatte
streiten (in Zimmerlautstärke)
Tancredi und Clorinda.

Später streicheln wir uns gewöhnlich. .

SCENIC MADRIGAL

That separates.
However close we lie,
fishes from other shores
swim where we thought
we were on solid ground.

Similarly deceived, outside, the thing
which (even now) we call society takes its course:
women who stand up for themselves like a man,
blubbery men,
animals that leave no trace and no address.

On our long-playing record
a (low-volume) quarrel takes place
between Tancredi and Clorinda.

Later we fondle each other.

FROM

Der Butt

1977

GESTILLT

Die Brust meiner Mutter war groß und weiß.
Den Zitzen anliegen.
Schmarotzen, bevor sie Flasche und Nuckel wird.
Mit Stottern, Komplexen drohen,
wenn sie versagt werden sollte.
Nicht nur quengeln.

Klare Fleischbrühe läßt die Milch einschießen
oder Sud aus Dorschköpfen trüb gekocht,
bis Fischaugen blind
ungefähr Richtung Glück rollen.

Männer nähren nicht.
Männer schielen heimwärts, wenn Kühe
mit schwerem Euter die Straße
und den Berufsverkehr sperren.
Männer träumen die dritte Brust.
Männer neiden dem Säugling
und immer fehlt ihnen.

Unsere bärtigen Brustkinder,
die uns steuerpflichtig versorgen,
schmatzen in Pausen zwischen Terminen,
an Zigaretten gelehnt.

Ab vierzig sollten alle Männer wieder gesäugt werden:
öffentlich und gegen Gebühr,
bis sie ohne Wunsch satt sind und nicht mehr weinen,
auf dem Klo weinen müssen: allein.

COMFORTED

My mother's breast was big and white.
Snuggle up to the teats.
Batten, before it turns into bottle and rubber.
Threaten a stammer, complexes,
if it should be withheld.
Whining is not enough.

A clear meat broth lets the milk jet in
or a stock of cods' heads boiled till it's murky
until fish eyes, blind,
roll off in the vague direction of bliss.

Men do not nourish.
Men squint homeward when cows
with heavy udders obstruct
the road and rush-hour traffic.
Men dream of the third breast.
Men envy the suckling infant
and always feel deprived.

Our bearded breast-fed babies
who, taxable, earn our keep,
smack their lips in lulls between engagements
while they lean on cigarettes.

After forty all men should be suckled again:
publicly, at a fixed price,
till they are comforted, wishless, and needn't cry anymore,
cry in the john, alone.

DEMETER

Mit offenem Auge
erkennt die Göttin,
wie blind der Himmel ist.

Rings werfen Wimpern versteinert Schatten.
Kein Lid will fallen und Schlaf machen.

Immer Entsetzen,
seitdem sie den Gott
hier auf dem Brachfeld sah,
wo die Pflugschar gezeugt wurde.

Rundum ist das Maultier willig über der Gerste.
Das ändert sich nicht.

Wir, aus dem Kreis gefallen,
machen ein Foto
überbelichtet.

DEMETER

With her eyes open
the goddess recognizes
how blind is heaven.

Around her, eyelashes, petrified, cast shadows.
No lid will drop and make sleep.

Always horror
since she saw the god
here, on the fallow field
where the plowshare was conceived.

All around the mule is willing over its barley.
That does not change.

We, fallen out of the cycle,
take a photograph,
overexposed.

WIE ICH MICH SEHE

Spiegelverkehrt und deutlicher schief.
Schon überlappen die oberen Lider.
Das eine Auge hängt müde, verschlagen das andere wach.
Soviel Einsicht und Innerei,
nachdem ich laut wiederholt
die Macht und ihren Besitz verbellt habe.
(Wir werden! Es wird! Das muß!)

Seht die porigen Backen.
Noch oder wieder: Federn blase ich leicht
und behaupte, was schwebt.
Wissen möchte das Kinn, wann es zittern darf endlich.
Dicht hält die Stirn; dem Ganzen fehlt ein Gedanke.
Wo, wenn das Ohr verdeckt ist
oder an andere Bilder verliehen,
nistet in Krümeln Gelächter?

Alles verschattet und mit Erfahrung verhängt.
Die Brille habe ich seitlich gelegt.
Nur aus Gewohnheit wittert die Nase.
Den Lippen,
die immer noch Federn blasen,
lese ich Durst ab.

Unterm Euter der schwarzweißen Kuh:
ich sehe mich trinken
oder dir angelegt, Köchin,

HOW I SEE MYSELF

Mirror-inverted and more clearly awry.
Already the upper eyelids overlap.
One eye hangs weary, the other cunning, alert.
So much insight and inwardness, after aloud
repeatedly I had barked at power and its property.
(We shall! It will! It must!)

Look at those porous cheeks.
Still or again, feathers I blow with ease
and assert that which hovers.
The chin wants to know when at last it may tremble.
It's the forehead that holds you together, the whole lacks a thought.
Where, when the ear is covered
or lent to other pictures,
does laughter nestle in crumbs?

Everything overshadowed and veiled with experience.
I have tilted the spectacles to one side.
Only from habit the nose catches a scent.
From the lips
that blow feathers still
I read thirst.

Under the black and white cow's udder:
I see myself drink
or sucking from you, cook,

nachdem deine Brust
tropfend über dem garenden Fisch hing;
du findest mich schön.

after your breast
had hung dripping over the boiling fish;
you think me handsome.

AM ENDE

Männer, die mit bekanntem Ausdruck
zu Ende denken,
schon immer zu Ende gedacht haben;
Männer, denen nicht Ziele—womöglich mögliche—
sondern das Endziel—die entsorgte Gesellschaft—
hinter Massengräbern den Pflock gesteckt hat;
Männer, die aus der Summe datierter Niederlagen
nur einen Schluß ziehen: den rauchverhangenen Endsieg
auf gründlich verbrannter Erde;
Männer, wie sie auf einer der täglichen Konferenzen,
nachdem sich das Gröbste als technisch machbar erwies,
die Endlösung beschließen,
sachlich männlich beschlossen haben;
Männer mit Überblick,
denen Bedeutung nachläuft,
große verstiegene Männer,
die niemand, kein warmer Pantoffel
hat halten können,
Männer mit steiler Idee, der Taten platt folgten,
sind endlich—fragen wir uns—am Ende?

AT THE END

Men who, as the saying goes,
think a thing to the end,
have always thought a thing to the end;
men for whom not aims—possibly possible ones—
but the final aim—a worry-free society—
sets up the winning-post behind mass graves;
men, who from the aggregate of dated setbacks
draw one conclusion: the smoke-blurred final victory
on thoroughly scorched earth;
men who at one of the daily meetings,
when the coarsest thing has proved technically feasible,
resolve on the final solution,
have resolved on it with a manly pragmatism;
men with an overall vision,
whom importance dogs;
great extravagant men
whom no one, no hearth-warmed slipper
has been able to hold,
men with a steep idea that's followed flatly by actions,
at last—we wonder—have come to the end?

ZUVIEL

Zwischen den Feiertagen,
sobald es spät still genug ist,
lese ich Orwells utopischen Roman »1984«,
den ich 1949 zum erstenmal
ganz anders gelesen habe.

Beiseite, neben dem Nußknacker und dem Päckchen Tabak,
liegt ein statistisches Buch,
dessen Zahlen die Weltbevölkerung,
wie sie ernährt—nicht ernährt wird,
bis zum Jahre 2000 steigern—verknappen.
In Pausen,
wenn ich nach meinem Tabak greife
oder eine Haselnuß knacke,
holen mich Schwierigkeiten ein,
die im Vergleich mit Big Brother
und dem globalen Eiweißmangel
klein sind,
aber nicht aufhören wollen, privat zu kichern.

Jetzt lese ich über Verhörmethoden in naher Zukunft.
Jetzt will ich mir Zahlen merken:
gegenwärtige Mortalitätsmuster
der Kindersterblichkeit in Südasien.
Jetzt zerfaser ich von den Rändern her,
weil vor den Feiertagen das nachgelassene Gezänk
in Päckchen verschnürt wurde: Ilsebills Wünsche . . .

TOO MUCH

Between the festivities,
as soon as it's late enough, quiet,
I read Orwell's utopian novel *1984,*
which I first read in 1949
quite differently.

Nearby, next to the nutcracker and the tobacco packet,
lies a statistical book
whose figures simplify the world population—
how it's fed, or not fed,
up to the year 2000.
At intervals,
when I reach for my tobacco
or crack a hazelnut,
problems catch up with me
which, compared to Big Brother
and the global protein shortage,
are small
but won't give up their private tittering.

Now I read about methods of interrogation in the near future.
Now I want to memorize figures:
current mortality patterns
among children in the Far East,
now from the edges I start unpicking—
because before the festivities our abated rows
were tied up with string in boxes—Ilsebill's wishes . . .

Zur Hälfte füllen Nußschalen den Aschenbecher.
Das ist zuviel alles.
Etwas muß gestrichen werden: Indien
oder der Oligarchische Kollektivismus
oder die familiäre Weihnacht.

Nutshells half fill the ashtray.
That's too much, all of it.
Something has to be cut, India
or our Oligarchic Collectivism
or our family Christmas.

ALLE BEIDE

Er sagt nicht meine, die Frau sagt er.
Die Frau will das nicht.
Das muß ich erst mit der Frau besprechen.

Angst zum Krawattenknoten gezurrt.
Angst, nachhause zu kommen.
Angst, zuzugeben.
Verängstigt sind beide einander Besitz.

Die Liebe klagt ihre Ansprüche ein.
Und das gewohnte Küßchen danach.
Nur noch Gedächtnis zählt.
Beide leben vom Streitwert.
(Die Kinder merken vorm Schlüsselloch was
und beschließen für später das Gegenteil.)

Aber, sagt er, ohne die Frau hätte ich nicht soviel.
Aber, sagt sie, er tut, was er kann und noch mehr.
Ein Segen, der Fluch, und als Fluch Gesetz wurde.
Ein Gesetz, das immer sozialer wird.
Zwischen den Einbauschränken, die abgezahlt sind,
bildet der Haß
Knötchen im Teppich: nicht pflegeleicht.

Beide entdecken einander,
wenn sie sich fremd genug sind,
nur noch im Kino.

BOTH

He says not my, the wife, he says.
The wife doesn't like that.
I must ask the wife what she thinks.

Fear pulled tight into a necktie knot.
Fear of getting home.
Fear of admitting.
In fear each belongs to the other.

Love files a suit for its claims.
And after that the usual peck.
Now only memory counts.
Both live on the sum in dispute.
(The kids at the keyhole get wind of something
and resolve to be different later.)

But, says he, without the wife I'd be worse off.
But, says she, he does what he can, and more.
A blessing, that curse, and when that curse became law.
A law that grows more and more social.
Between the built-in cupboards, with the last installment paid off,
hatred forms
tangled lumps in the carpet: not easy to clean.

Each discovers the other
when they feel distant enough—
at the movies only, these days.

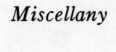

Miscellany

DIE LÜGE

Ihre rechte Schulter hängt,
sagte mein Schneider.
Weil ich rechts die Schultasche trug,
sagte ich und errötete.

THE LIE

Your right shoulder droops,
said my tailor.
Because I carried my school satchel
on the right, I said, blushing.

TODESARTEN

Du hast sie gesammelt:
Schränke voll,
deine Aussteuer.

In leichteren Zeiten, als das noch anging
und die Metapher auf ihren Freipaß pochte,
wäre dir (rettend) ein Hörspiel gelungen,
in dem jener typisch doppelbödige Trödler,
durch dich vergöttert, alte Todesarten verliehen
neue aufgekauft hätte.

Bedrängt von.
Keine kam dir zu nah.
So scheu warst du nicht.
Wichsende Knaben hatten den Vorhang gelöchert:
jeder sah alles, Seide und chemische Faser,
die jüngste Kollektion, bezügliche Zitate.

Todesarten: außer den windigen Kleidchen
diese probieren und diese;
die letzte paßte.

(Als Ingeborg Bachmann starb)

KINDS OF DEATH

You collected them:
wardrobesful,
your dowry.

In easier times, when that was still in the cards
and metaphors bragged about their special passes,
you'd have brought off a (saving) radio play
in which that typically two-faced peddler
you deified would have dealt out old kinds of death
and bought up new ones.

Hard-pressed by.
None molested you.
You were not that shy.
Masturbating boys had punched holes in the curtains:
each one saw it all, silk and chemical fiber
the latest collection, relevant quotations.

Kinds of death: apart from the flimsy small dresses
try on this one and this one;
the last one fitted.

                                   (when Ingeborg Bachmann died)

SARGNÄGEL

Woran ich mich halte,
wovon ich nicht lasse,
was an der Lippe mir hängt,
weshalb ich mit Rauchzeichen
mich beweise: Seht!

Noch lebt es, kringelt sich,
speichert Rückstände,
hält seinen Traum wach
und will sich verbrauchen,
wie da geschrieben steht
und aus Asche zu lesen ist:
Worte am Kreuz.

Seine Sargnägel (sieben)
aus anderer Zeitweil,
handgeschmiedet und kürzlich wiedergefunden,
als der Friedhof nahbei, weil außer Betrieb
(und neuzugewinnender Parkplätze wegen),
gründlich planiert wurde.

Deshalb rauche ich
gegen jede Vernunft.

COFFIN NAILS

That to which I cling,
that I never cease from,
that which hangs on my lips,
that for which with smoke signals
I prove myself: look!

Still it's alive, still curls,
stores up arrears,
keeps its dream awake
and wants to use itself up
as it is written
and to be read from ashes:
words on the cross.

His coffin nails (seven)
from a different provisional era,
handmade and found again lately,
when the nearby graveyard, because out of use
(and for the sake of new parking lots),
was thoroughly bulldozed.

That's why I smoke
in the teeth of all reason.

MEIN SCHUH

Mit ihm zerstritten.
Läuft gegenläufig davon.
Kommt flüchtig entgegen.

Mütze trifft Schuh:
Auswärts sie, heimwärts er.
Beide auf Abschied gedellt:
vergriffen vergangen.

Allseits mein Schuh.
Wem ich entlaufen, was mich eingeholt,
lese ich seiner Sohle ab:

Als ich noch barfuß.
Als mir kein Senkel aufgehen wollte.
Als ich mir witzig daneben stand.
Als er noch knarrte, anstößig ich.

Und die Geschichte der Köchin in mir,
wie sie für General Rapp (weil die Franzosen)
jenen knolligen Pilz fein in die Suppe.
Aber er aß nicht.
Nur seine Gäste.
Unter denen Graf Posadovski.
Dessen Stiefel sie später.

Da kommen gelaufen: das Schwein und sein Leder.
Wie gehts?—Auf und ab.

MY SHOE

Fallen out with it.
Contrarily runs away.
Fleetingly comes toward me.

Cap encounters shoe:
Outward bound the one, homeward the other.
Both pinched for departure:
handled down walked out.

On all sides my shoe.
From whom I ran away, what caught up with me,
I read from the sole:

When I went barefoot.
When no lace would untie for me.
When I stood next to me, witty.
When it still creaked, I a scandal.

And the history of the cook in me,
how for General Rapp (because the French)
she chopped up that bulbous fungus for the soup.
But he didn't eat.
Only his guests.
Among them, Count Posadovski.
Whose boots she later.

Here they come running, the pig and its leather.
How's it going?—up and down.

Fünf mal sechs.
Die Unruhe ausschreiten.
Stühle scheuen.

Nicht pfeifen, weil ja kein Wald
und die Angst möbliert.
Den Schuh ermüden.

Oder auf langer Stange rund um den Platz
oder ihm Wurzeln einreden
oder vom großen Auslauf träumen.

Schon auf Strümpfen geh ich dem Faden nach,
sammel, was blieb: Standpunkte
aus der Familie der Kopffüßler:
mittlerweile verkrautet.

Five times six.
To pace one's restlessness.
Avoid chairs.

Not whistle, there being no forest,
and fear is furnished.
Tire out the shoe.

Or round the square on a long pole
or talk it into roots
or dream of the great takeoff.

In my socks already I follow the thread,
collect what's left: standpoints
of the species cephalopod:
gone to seed meanwhile.

MÜLL UNSER

Suchte Steine und fand
den überlebenden Handschuh
aus synthetischer Masse.

Jeder Fingerling sprach.
Nein, nicht die dummen Seglergeschichten,
sondern was bleiben wird:

Müll unser
Strände lang.
Während abhanden wir
niemand Verlust sein werden.

OUR LITTER WHICH

Looked for pebbles and found
the surviving glove
made of synthetic pulp.

Every finger spoke.
No, not those daft yachtman's yarns
but of what will remain:

our litter
beaches long.
While we, mislaid,
will be nobody's loss.

ABSCHIED NEHMEN

Mir träumte, ich müßte Abschied nehmen
von allen Dingen, die mich umstellt haben
und ihren Schatten werfen: die vielen besitzanzeigenden
Fürwörter. Abschied vom Inventar, dieser Liste
diverser Fundsachen. Abschied
von den ermüdenden Düften,
den Gerüchen, mich wachzuhalten, von der Süße,
der Bitternis, vom Sauren an sich
und von der hitzigen Schärfe des Pfefferkorns.
Abschied vom Ticktack der Zeit, vom Ärger am Montag,
dem schäbigen Mittwochsgewinn, vom Sonntag
und dessen Tücke, sobald Langeweile Platz nimmt.
Abschied von allen Terminen: was zukünftig
fällig sein soll.

Mir träumte, ich müßte von jeder Idee, ob tot
oder lebend geboren, vom Sinn, der den Sinn
hinterm Sinn sucht,
und von der Dauerläuferin Hoffnung auch
mich verabschieden. Abschied vom Zinseszins
der gesparten Wut, vom Erlös gespeicherter Träume,
von allem, was auf Papier steht, erinnert zum Gleichnis,
als Roß und Reiter Denkmal wurde. Abschied
von allen Bildern, die sich der Mensch gemacht hat.
Abschied vom Lied, dem gereimten Jammer, Abschied
von den geflochtenen Stimmen, vom Jubel sechschörig,
dem Eifer der Instrumente,
von Gott und Bach.

LEAVE-TAKING

I dreamed that I must take leave
of all the things that surrounded me
and cast their shadows: all those possessive
pronouns. And of the inventory, list
of diverse things found. Take leave
of the wearying odors,
smells, to keep me awake, of sweetness,
of bitterness, of sourness per se
and the peppercorn's fiery sharpness.
Take leave of time's ticktock, of Monday's annoyance,
Wednesday's shabby gains, of Sunday
and its treacheries, as soon as boredom sits down.
Take leave of all deadlines: of what in the future
is to be due.

I dreamed that of every idea, whether stillborn
or live, of the sense that looks
for the sense behind sense,
and of the long-distance runner hope as well
I must take leave. Take leave of the compound interest
of saved-up fury, the proceeds of stored dreams,
of all that's written on paper, recalled as analogy
when horse and rider became a memorial. Take leave
of all the images men have made for themselves.
Take leave of the song, rhymed bellyaching, and of
voices that interweave, that six-part jubilation,
the fervor of instruments,
of God and of Bach.

Mir träumte, ich müßte Abschied nehmen
vom kahlen Geäst,
von den Wörtern Knospe, Blüte und Frucht,
von den Zeiten des Jahres, die ihre Stimmungen
satt haben und auf Abschied bestehen.
Frühnebel. Spätsommer. Wintermantel. April April! rufen,
noch einmal Herbstzeitlose und Märzbecher sagen,
Dürre Frost Schmelze.
Den Spuren im Schnee davonlaufen. Vielleicht
sind zum Abschied die Kirschen reif. Vielleicht
spielt der Kuckuck verrückt und ruft. Noch einmal
Erbsen aus Schoten grün springen lassen. Oder
die Pusteblume: jetzt erst begreife ich, was sie will.

Ich träumte, ich müßte von Tisch, Tür und Bett
Abschied nehmen und den Tisch, die Tür und das Bett
belasten, weit öffnen, zum Abschied erproben.
Mein letzter Schultag: ich buchstabiere die Namen
der Freunde und sage ihre Telefonnummern auf: Schulden
sind zu begleichen; ich schreibe zum Schluß meinen Feinden
ein Wort: Schwamm drüber—oder:
Es lohnte den Streit nicht.
Auf einmal habe ich Zeit.
Es sucht mein Auge, als sei es geschult worden,
Abschied zu nehmen, rundum Horizonte, die Hügel
hinter den Hügeln, die Stadt
auf beiden Seiten des Flusses ab,
als müßte erinnert verschont gerettet werden, was
auf der Hand liegt: zwar aufgegeben, doch immer noch
dinglich, hellwach.

I dreamed that I must take leave
of bare branchwork,
of the words bud, blossom and fruit,
of the seasons that, sick of their moods,
insist on departure.
Early mist, late summer. Winter coat. Call out: April April!
say again autumn crocus and May tree,
drought frost thaw.
Run away from tracks in the snow. Perhaps
when I go the cherries will be ripe. Perhaps
the cuckoo will act mad and call. Once more
let peas jump green from their pods. Or the
dandelion clock: only now do I grasp what it wants.

I dreamed that of table, door and bed
I must take leave and put a strain on
table, door and bed, open them wide, test them in going.
My last schoolday: I spell out the names
of my friends and recite their telephone numbers: debts
are to be settled: last of all I write to my enemies
briefly: let bygones be bygones—or:
It wasn't worth quarreling over.
Suddenly I have time.
My eyes as though they'd been trained
in leave-taking, search horizons all around, the hills
behind the hills, the city
on either bank of the river,
as though what goes without saying
must be remembered preserved saved: given up, true, but still
palpable, wide-awake.

Mir träumte, ich müßte Abschied nehmen
von dir, dir und dir, von meinem Ungenügen,
dem restlichen Ich: was hinterm Komma blieb
und kümmert seit Jahren.
Abschied von sattsam vertrauter Fremde,
von den Gewohnheiten, die sich Recht geben höflich,
von unserem eingeschrieben verbrieften Haß. Nichts
war mir näher als deine Kälte. So viel Liebe genau
falsch erinnert. Am Ende
war alles versorgt: Sicherheitsnadeln zuhauf.
Bleibt noch der Abschied von deinen Geschichten,
die immer das Bollwerk, den Dampfer suchen,
der von Stralsund, aus der brennenden Stadt
beladen mit Flüchtlingen kommt;
und Abschied von meinen Gläsern, die Scherben, allzeit
nur Scherben, sich selbst als Scherben
im Sinn hatten. Nein,
keine Kopfstände mehr.

Und nie wieder Schmerz. Nichts,
dem Erwartung entgegenliefe. Dieses Ende
ist Schulstoff, bekannt. Dieser Abschied
wurde in Kursen geübt. Seht nur, wie billig
Geheimnisse nackt sind! Kein Geld zahlt Verrat mehr aus.
Zu Schleuderpreisen des Feindes entschlüsselte Träume.
Endlich hebt sich der Vorteil auf, macht uns
die Schlußrechnung gleich,
siegt zum letzten Mal die Vernunft,
ist ohne Unterschied alles,
was einen Odem führt, alles, was kreucht

I dreamed that I must take leave
of you, you and you, of my insufficiency,
the residual self: what remained behind the comma
and for years has rankled.
Take leave of the familiar strangeness we live with,
of the habits that politely justify themselves
of the bonded and registered hatred between us. Nothing
was closer to me than your coldness. So much love recalled
with precise wrongness. In the end
everything had been seen to: safety pins galore.
Lastly, the leave-taking from your stories
that always look for the bulwark, the steamer
out of Stralsund, the city on fire,
laden with refugees;
take leave of my glassware that had shards in mind,
only shards at all times, shards
of itself. Not that:
no more headstands.

And no more pain, ever. Nothing
that expectation might run to meet. This end
is classroom stuff, stale. This leave-taking
was crammed for in courses. Just look how cheaply
secrets go naked! Betrayal pays out no more money.
Decoded dreams of the enemy, at cut-rate prices.
At last advantage cancels itself, evens out for us
the balance sheet,
reason triumphs for the last time,
leveling
all that has breath, all things that creep

und fleucht, alles, was noch
ungedacht und was werden sollte vielleicht,
am Ende und scheidet aus.

Doch als mir träumte, ich müßte
von jeglicher Kreatur, damit von keinem Getier,
dem einst Noah die Arche gezimmert,
Nachgeschmack bliebe, Abschied nehmen sofort,
träumte ich nach dem Fisch, dem Schaf und dem Huhn,
die mit dem Menschengeschlecht alle vergingen,
eine einzelne Ratte mir, die warf neun Junge
und hatte Zukunft für sich.

or fly, all that had not yet
been thought and was to be perhaps,
at an end, on its way out.

But when I dreamed that I must
take leave at once of all creation
so that of no animal for which Noah once
built the ark there should be a redolence,
after the fish, the sheep and the hen
that all perished together with humankind,
I dreamed for myself one rat that gave birth to nine
and was blessed with a future.

Novemberland

1993

DAS UNSRE

Breit liegt das Land, in dessen Lied wie in Prospekten
sich Schönheit weit gehügelt austrägt, gegen Norden flach,
besiedelt, eng (in dieser Zeit) bis unters Dach.
Wo sich die Kinder einst vor Vaters Zorn versteckten,

ist keine Zuflucht mehr, nein, nichts schließt mehr geheim.
So offen sind wir kenntlich, allseits ausgestellt,
daß jeder Nachbar, ringsum alle Welt
als Unglück treiben sieht, was unsres Glückes Keim.

Wo wir uns finden, hat verkehrte Konjunktur
uns fett gemacht. Dank Leid und Kummer satt,
schlug mästend Elend an als freien Marktes Kur;
und selbst auf unsre Sünden gab's Rabatt.
Still liegt Novemberland, verflucht zum tugendhaften Fleiß,
in Angst vorm Jüngstgericht, dem überhöhten Preis.

WHAT'S OURS

Broad lies the land whose anthem like its brochure pages
a beauty widely hillocked fills, toward the north more flat,
all peopled, densely (now) up to each attic slat.
Where children used to hide from Father's cruel rages

no refuge now remains, no secret lock in need.
So well we advertise, exhibit with such pride
that every neighbor, all the world outside
sees as disaster's shoot what we call happy seed.

Where now we find ourselves, a specious boom of shares
had fattened us. With grief and suffering sated,
a force-fed misery peddled free-market wares;
and at a discount our worst sins were rated.
Hushed lies Novemberland, condemned to virtuous sweat
for fear of Judgment Day, inflation gross and net.

NOVEMBERLAND

Da komm ich her. Das feiert jährlich alle Neune.
Von dem ich weg will über selbsterdachte Zäune,
doch in verkehrten Schuhen dahin laufe, wo ich heiße
und ruchbar bin für die zurückgelaßne Scheiße.

Das bleibt veränderlich sich gleich
und ähnelt unterm Schutt der Moden—
mal sind es Jeans, dann wieder Loden—
den abgelebten Fotos aus dem Dritten Reich.

Novembertote, laßt sie ruhn!
Wir haben mit uns Lebenden genug zu tun.
Doch diese sind nicht jene, jene sind erwacht
und haben sich als Täter das gleiche ähnlich ausgedacht.
Nicht abgebucht noch steuerfrei ist der Gewinn
aus Schuldenlast, für die ich haftbar bin.

NOVEMBERLAND

That's where I'm from. That yearly celebrates every nine.*
That's what I wish to leave, cross fences never mine
but in the wrong shoes run to where I'm part of it
and am responsible for the residuous shit.

That changeably remains the same,
beneath the trash of trends is like—
now blue jeans, now green loden are the name of the game—
faded, discarded photos from our late Third Reich.

November's dead, leave them alone!
For us who live there's quite enough now to be done.
But these are not the others, those have now awoken,
thought up the same as doers by the self-same token.
Not written off nor tax free is the profit made
from debts that now by my sort must be paid.

---

* [*Translator's note*: An allusion not only to the game of skittles, in which nine is the top
score, but to Hitler's *putsch* in 1923, the *Kristallnacht* of 1938, and the end of the Berlin
Wall in 1989, all of which occurred on November 9.]

SPÄTE SONNENBLUMEN

November schlug sie, schwarz in schwarz vor Hell.
Noch ragen Strünke, sind der Farben Spott,
im Regen schräg und suchen sich Vergleiche,
auch Reime, etwa Gott und Leiche.

Noch immer tauglich, stehn sie mir Modell,
weil ausgesägt vor Himmeln, deren Grau
im Ausschnitt und total zerfließt,
drauf eine Meldung sich als Botschaft liest:

Geschieden sind wie Mann und Frau
nach kurzer Ehe Land und Leute.
Karg war die Ernte, reich die Beute.
Ach, Treuhand hat uns abgeschöpft.
Wer bei Verdacht schon Sonnenblumen köpft,
dem werden Zeugen fehlen, den erwischt die Meute.

LATE SUNFLOWERS

November struck them, black in black on bright.
Still the stalks loom, mocking all colors' lapse,
askew in rain, look for analogies
and rhymes, like God perhaps, corpse or disease.

Still good for something, as my models right,
because, sawn out against skies whose listless gray
in detail and the whole is blurred,
on them this message, copied word for word:

As wife from husband, briefly wed,
people from country break away.
Harvest was poor, the booty ample.
Oh, the Trustee* has ruined us.
He who beheads the sunflowers, merely suspicious,
will find no witnesses, him the pack will trample.

---

* [*Translator's note*: The *Treuhand*, a body of government-appointed receivers whose function was to privatize formerly state-owned property in the former GDR].

ALLERSEELEN

Ich flog nach Polen, nahm November mit.
Die Frage, was, wenn polnisch meine Zunge
mir wörtlich wäre und tödlich folgsam beim Ulanenritt—
ich rauchte tief katholisch und auf Lunge—,

blieb wortreich ohne Antwort, deutsch auf deutsch vernarrt:
Zwar schmeichle der Gedanke, sei bizarr, apart,
doch müsse ich bei heimischer Kontrolle
zu Markte tragen meine eingefärbte Wolle.

So nachbarlich durchnäßt, so ferngerückt verloren,
so anverwandt vom Lied und Leid im Lied besessen,
so heimlich zugetan, doch taub auf beiden Ohren,
sind Freunde wir, bis Schmerz, weil nie vergessen
die Narbe (unsre) pocht; umsonst war alles Hoffen:
Die Gräber alle stehn auf Allerseelen offen.

ALL SOULS

I flew to Poland, November at my side.
The question was, if Polish there my tongue
were literal and deadly in obedience when the Ulans ride—
Catholic deep down I smoked, down to the lung—

stayed voluble with no answer, German to German fixed:
The quirk might flatter, because so quaintly mixed.
Yet on returning to the home control
to market I must carry still my dyed-in wool.

So soaked in neighborliness, so far astray for years,
so much akin to song and grief possessed in song,
so secretly inclined, yet deaf now in both ears,
we're friends till pain, remembered for so long,
the scar (our own) will throb; all hoping was in vain:
All Souls' Day opens each and every grave again.

STURMWARNUNG

Im Radio angekündigt, kam von England ein Orkan.
Nur wenig Tote diesmal, überhoch die Schäden
an Sachen, Material, von Klimasorgen nicht zu reden:
Die Stürme könnten, wie der allgemeine Wahn,

sich mehren, bis matt wir sind von einheitlicher Last
und ausgeschlossen wären aus dem Club der Reichen,
denn selbst die D-Mark ließe sich erweichen,
wenn zügelloses Wetter dauerhaft als Gast

hier heimisch wünscht zu werden, wie der Fremden Flut,
die frech, trotz Drogensucht und aidsverseuchtem Blut,
mit uns sich mischen möchte, will uns trüb durchrassen,
so daß wir sie, nicht uns mehr hassen.—
Schon wieder, angekündigt, ein Orkan zuviel,
der keine Grenzen kennt, klopft an und fordert laut Asyl.

GALE WARNING

Forecast on radio, from England a hurricane blew.
Not many dead this time, the damage far too great
in things, material, fears for our climate's state:
that gales, like our delusion, general madness, too,

could now increase until, enfeebled by a common load,
we could be dropped and banned from affluence's club
because the D-mark even could receive a rub
if unreined weather for its permanent abode

chose ours, imposed itself, like all that foreign flood
that, brash in drug addiction, AIDS-infected blood,
desires to mix with us, to miscegenate,
so that it's them, no more ourselves, we hate.
And, forecast, yet another most unwelcome such
gate-crashes every frontier, loudmouthed. It's too much.

VORM ERSTEN ADVENT

Was teuer wird: das Leben, der Kredit, Benzin!
Im kahlen Garten spärlich Hagebutten glühn.
Auf allgemeinem Grau ein Farbenklecks
erinnert uns an Ehestreit und sommerlichen Sex.

So abgefackelt nach nur bißchen Lustgewinn
krümmt sich Novemberland, bekümmert vom Gebrüll:
kein Penis mehr, doch tausendmal ein Skin
steht für Gewalt und unversorgten Müll.

Der gilt als schlau, der rechnet in Prozenten
den fremden Anteil nach bei deutschen Renten,
als könnte jenen eine Rechnung dienen,
die schweigend grinsen hinter den Gardinen,
wenn draußen Mölln ist, unsre kleine Stadt,
die sich ganz unverhofft ein Fest bereitet hat.

BEFORE THE FIRST SUNDAY IN ADVENT

What's growing costly: living, credit, gasoline!
In the stripped garden sparsely rosehips cast their sheen.
Against the general grayness a few flecks
remind us of our marriage tiffs and summer sex.

So, all burned off, burned out, with little lust thrown in,
Novemberland writhes, by uproar cowed, dejected:
no penis now, but, thousandfold, a skin
stands for new violence, rubbish not collected.

Cunning they think the one who in percents
works out the foreign share in German pensions,
as though by calculation those could win
who silent behind curtains wait and grin,
when it is Mölln* outside, our little town
that to a quite unhoped-for fête gets down.

* [*Translator's note*: The site of atrocities committed against foreigners by neo-Nazis in 1992].

AUSSER PLAN

Auf alte Zeitung, die im Garten treibt, unstetig,
und sich an Dornen reißt, auf Suche nach Ästhetik,
schlägt wütig Gegenwart, ein rüder Hagelschauer;
November spottet aller Schönschrift Dauer.

Schaut nur, die blassen stilgerechten Knaben,
die sich, auf Wunsch, der Stunde Null verschrieben haben.
Jetzt jammern sie, weil selbst auf Stasispitzel
Verlaß nicht ist, um Zeilenschwund und momentanen Kitzel.

Betreten reisen sie, wie altgewohnt, zur nächsten Vernissage,
auf Spesen mürrisch von Premiere zu Premiere
und reden sich bei Billigsekt und Klatsch in Rage;
da kommt Gewalt dem fixen Wortfluß in die Quere
und brüllt aufs neue überlieferten Jargon:
verschreckt (ganz außer Plan) wacht auf das Feuilleton.

UNPLANNED

On an old daily drifting in the garden, jerkily,
that tears itself on thorns, in search of harmony,
the present, a rude hailstorm, beats thick and fast;
November mocks calligraphy's claim to last.

Just look at any pale, conformist, trendy boy
committed to the zero hour, which gave him joy.
His kind complain, since on no Stasi spy
they can rely now, columns shrink, the thrills run dry.

Sheepish but as of old, to the next vernissage
they travel, their expenses paid, to the next opening night,
with gossip, cheap champagne to fuel the old rage;
but violence breaks up the flow so smooth and bright,
roars out anew a jargon common once as dirt:
alarmed (and quite unplanned), the arts page leaps alert.

ANDAUERNDER REGEN

Die Angst geht um, November droht zu bleiben.
Nie wieder langer Tage Heiterkeit.
Die letzten Fliegen fallen von den Scheiben,
und Stillstand folgt dem Schnellimbiß der Zeit.

Des Bauherrn Ängste gründen sich auf Fundamente,
denn Pfusch von gestern könnte heut zutage treten.
Die Jugend bangt—schon früh vergreist—um ihre Rente.
Und auch des Volkes Diener üppige Diäten

sind ängstlich rasch verdoppelt worden.
Die Skins mit Schlips und Scheitel kriegen Orden.
Wer dieser Wirtschaft Zukunftsmärkte lobt,
den hat der Zeitgeist regelrecht gedopt,
dem steht Zweidrittelmehrheit stramm, aus Angst geeint;
ein Narr, der im Novemberregen weint.

PERSISTENT RAIN

November is here to stay, our fear of it makes plain.
Gone are the long days of unbroken brightness.
The last flies drop from each dull windowpane,
a standstill has replaced time's fast-food lightness.

The property owner's fears are based on real foundations,
since yesterday's botching could come to light today.
Young people—prematurely aged—to pension cares fall prey.
Also, the civil servants' rich remunerations

in anxious haste were doubled by the boards.
Skinheads with ties and partings get awards.
Who praises this economy's market hope
is one the zeitgeist thoroughly could dope,
him a (fear-forged) two-thirds' majority guards in vain;
a fool who'll weep in the November rain.

DIE FESTUNG WÄCHST

Liegt brach das Land zum Fraß der Krähenschar.
Der Maulwurf mehrt sich, und verdächtig häufig
sind längs den Zäunen fremde Hunde läufig.
Wir sollen zahlen: auf die Hand und bar.

Weil in der Mitte liegend, reich und ungeschützt,
hat planend Furcht ein Bauwerk ausgeschwitzt:
als Festung will Novemberland sich sicher machen
vor Roma, Schwarzen, Juden und Fellachen.

Nach Osten hin soll Polen Grenzmark sein;
so schnell fällt nützlich uns Geschichte ein.
Das Burgenbauen war schon immer unsre Lust,
den Wall zu ziehn, die Mauer zu errichten,
und gegen Festungskoller, Stumpfsinn, Lagerfrust
half stets ein Hölderlin im Brotsack mit Gedichten.

THE FORTRESS GROWS

The land lies fallow, food now for rooks and crows.
The moles proliferate and, as they'd never done,
suspect, along the fences strange dogs run.
We are to pay: in cash, and through the nose.

Because mid-European, wealthy and vulnerable,
fear sweated out its drafts for a defensive wall:
now as a fortress Novemberland seeks to be
safe from Black, Fellah, Jew, Turk, Romany.

As eastern border Poland will serve again:
so fast we think of history, to our gain.
Building of castles has always been our special joy,
to raise the rampart, excavate the moat;
and against fortress megrims, dullness, gloom attacks
always a Hölderlin helped with poems in our packs.

ENTLAUBT

Der Nußbaum leer, hat alles fallenlassen.
Die Körbe schwer, aus schwarzem Schalenbrei
zieh Tinten ich, die Unschuld, die sich weiß beteuert, hassen.
Aus bittrem Sud fließt meine Litanei.

Was wirft hier Blasen, sprengt Beton,
der unsren Parkplatz überm kommunalen Sumpf
so sicher machte? Gehegte Ordnung jeglicher Fasson
ist außer Kurs, und Glieder, ledig, ohne Rumpf,

sind unterwegs, im Gleichschritt wie geübt.
Gestreckte Arme grüßen irgendwas.
Drauf ein Gebrüll, das nur sein Echo liebt,
aus Köpfen, die gedunsen sind vom Haß,
bis daß—Pen, Krach!, welch komisch echter Knall . . .
Komm! Laß uns Nüsse knacken nach dem jüngsten Fall.

DEFOLIATED

The nut tree has dropped all, defoliate.
The baskets heavy, from black husk cellulose
inks I extract that for the innocence professing whiteness renders
   hate.
From bitter broth of pulp my litany flows.

What throws up bubbles, blasts the concrete face
that made our car park over communal bogs
so safe? All sorts of order formerly in place
are out of currency, and trunkless limbs like logs

are on the march, in practiced unison.
Extended arms salute a who knows what.
Then a great roar that loves its echo alone
from heads all swollen with resentment, hate,
until—bang, crash—a lifelike, laughable pop . . .
Come on! Let's crack some nuts after the latest drop.

NACH KURZER KRANKHEIT

Verschnupft das Land, die Grippe sucht uns heim
und macht aufs Krippenkind sich einen Fieberreim.
Aktive Viren, wach zu neuem Kult,
den wir besänftigt glaubten, pfleglich eingelullt.

Bis uns die Augen triefen und der Blick getrübt,
verrotzt, weil nun auch Taschentücher fehlen,
wird alte Klage jung vertont geübt,
auf daß wir eine Stimme sind beim Hustentropfenzählen.

Kaum ausgeschwitzt, doch noch vom Brüllen heiser,
verhallt Gewalt, bellt leis und auf Verlangen leiser.
Kaum abgeklungen, schrumpft die Grippe zur Legende
und findet in der Talkshow prompt ihr gutes Ende:
ganz locker wird vom Hocker diskutiert,
warum der Mensch sich bei Gelegenheit vertiert.

AFTER BRIEF ILLNESS

All runny-nosed the land, the flu bug has run wild
and makes itself a rhyme upon the manger child.
Quick viruses, alert to the new cult
we thought assuaged long since, carefully soothed and lulled.

Till our eyes drip, our vision that was blurred
grows snotty too, with hankies scarce in shops,
old moans, set to new music, now are heard,
so that we form one voice while counting cough mixture drops.

Hardly yet sweated out, still hoarse with all that roar,
violence fades, barks softly and, if requested, more.
Hardly subsided, the flu shrinks to a legend
and in a talk show finds its happy ending:
quite glibly on their stools now they debate
why on occasion humans lapse from the human state.

BEI KLARER SICHT

Komm, Nebel, komm! Und mach uns anonym.
Wir sind ertappt auf frischer (unterlaßner) Tat.
Versalzen welkt nun unser harmloser Salat,
der treuherzig, wie einst Minister Blüm,

mit Gästen rechnete, für die brav andre zahlen.
So lebten wir begünstigt auf Kredit,
doch jemand, der (ein Gott?) am Nebelvorhang zieht,
verriet schon jetzt die Zahlen nächster Wahlen.

Fein rausgeputzt, verkürzt auf Mittelmaß,
der Riß verklebt, der Klassen gröbster Unterschied
bemäntelt. Kein Rüchlein (nein!) erinnerte ans Gas,
und nur die dritte Strophe galt (halbblau) im Lied.
Auf Siegers Seite lebten wir, behütet und getrennt,
bis uns die Einheit schlug, die keine Gnade kennt.

IN CLEAR PERSPECTIVE

Come, fog, o come! Make us anonymous.
We have been caught red-handed in the (undone) act.
Our salad wilts with too much of the salt it lacked,
as guileless as once Blüm, our Minister, was,

expecting guests that others pay for, raising no objections.
We lived on credit, privileged and certain,
but somebody (a God?) who lifts the long fog's curtain
has leaked the figures for the next elections.

Dressed up, all shortened to the medium size,
tears plastered over, class differences most crass
all cloaked. No whiff (oh no!) reminded them of gas.
The anthem's third stanza only valid (hummed with lowered eyes).
On the victor's side we lived, divided, safe from stress,
till unity struck us and proved merciless.

WER KOMMT?

Novemberschwärze vor verwaschnem Hell:
die letzten Sonnenblumen stehen schwarz Modell.
Seitab verglühen restlich Hagebutten.
Weil oben ohne, nässen Bäume ohne Kutten

gestaffelt und vereinzelt, auch der Nußbaum leer.
Fern übt mit Waffenschein ein einsames Gewehr.
Den häßlich kleinen Unterschied vertuscht der Nebel.
Ach, wüßt ich dem Adventsgebrüll doch einen Knebel.

Wer kommt, ist da, multipliziert?
Im Radio angekündigt, nur wie üblich, ein Orkan,
der seine Wut gewöhnlich unterwegs verliert.
Vor jähem Frost geschützt der blanke Wasserhahn,
verschnürt die Päckchen, fertig zum Versand;
demnächst droht Weihnacht dem Novemberland.

WHO'S COMING?

November blackness againt bright tints effete:
as models the last sunflowers blackly sit.
Beside them the residual rosehips fade.
Bare at the tops, trees, cowlless, drip and shed

what's left, in groups or single, even the nut tree bare.
A lonely gun that's licensed rehearses from afar.
Fog blots and blurs the ugly little doubt.
I wish I knew a gag, too, for the advent shout.

Who's coming, is here, and multiplied?
As usual the radio forecasts a mere hurricane
that usually on the way loses its force and stride.
The water tap's been lagged against sudden frost again,
the parcels are tied up, ready for mailing; and
imminent Christmas threatens our Novemberland.